SAN FRANCISCO
Portrait of a City

SAN FRANCISCO

Portrait of a City

LAWRENCE MIGDALE

GRAPHIC ARTS™ BOOKS

To my family: Terry, Dan, and Ari.
—LAWRENCE MIGDALE

Acknowledgments
Heartfelt thanks to Diane Hoyt-Goldsmith, Dana Roberts, and Ervin Grinberg
for all their help with creating the images in this book.
—L. M.

All photographs © MMVIII by Lawrence Migdale, except as noted below.
DanitaDelimont: page 35 by William Sutton, page 47 by David R. Frazier, pages 56 and 57 by
Mark Gibson, page 64 by Dennis Flaherty/Jaynes Gallery, page 106 by Inger Hogstrom;
IndexOpen: pages 2, 24–25, 31, 36–37, 38, and 54; iStock: page 7 by Daniel Cardiff, page 9 by
Jukeboxhero, page 30 by Craig Cozart, page 34 by Serge Surkov, page 39 by ZiMa, pages 40–41
and 99 by Can Balcioglu, page 55 by Dave Huss/Graphically Speaking, page 62 by
ObservePhoto.com, page 68–69 by Kent Steffens, and page 75 by David Becker.

Library of Congress Control Number: 2008927595
International Standard Book Number: 978-0-88240-750-0

Captions and book compilation © MMVIII by
Graphic Arts™ Books, an imprint of
Graphic Arts Center Publishing Company
P.O. Box 10306, Portland, Oregon 97296-0306
503/226-2402; www.gacpc.com
The five-dot logo is a registered trademark of
Graphic Arts Center Publishing Company.

President: Charles M. Hopkins
Associate Publisher: Douglas A. Pfeiffer
Editorial Staff: Timothy W. Frew, Kathy Howard, Jean Bond-Slaughter
Production Coordinator: Vicki Knapton
Design: Cover, Vicki Knapton; Interior, Jean Andrews

Printed in the United States of America

FRONT COVER: ● The Golden Gate Bridge, completed in 1937
at a cost of thirty-five million dollars, is an icon of San Francisco.
BACK COVER: ● A row of Victorian houses known as the Painted Ladies
faces Alamo Square Park, set on Telegraph Hill overlooking much of San Francisco.
◄◄ A cable car tops Hyde Street hill, with Alcatraz Island in the background.
◄ The Golden Gate Bridge, where San Francisco Bay meets the
Pacific Ocean, connects San Francisco and Marin County.
► A tulip garden embellishes Golden Gate Park.

◄ A Japanese tea garden
offers peace in Golden Gate Park.
▲ Two people paraglide together—called
tandem paragliding—over the beach at
Fort Funston, south of Ocean Beach.

◄ Alamo Square Park, comprising some six
city blocks, is lined by Victorian-style mansions.
▲ Called the Painted Ladies since the 1970s, the Alamo
mansions have been featured in movies,
television shows, and commercials.

▲ A bubble demonstration attracts
onlookers at San Francisco's Exploratorium, an
interactive museum of science, art, and human perception.
▶ The San Francisco Art Institute was founded in 1871.
▶▶ San Francisco's skyline features the Transamerica
Pyramid (left) at 853 feet and 555 California Street
(right) at 779 feet, the city's tallest buildings.

10

◄ Pacific Heights, an affluent San Francisco neighborhood,
offers panoramic views of the Bay, the Golden Gate Bridge, and Alcatraz.
▲ A container vessel passes the Marina, an upscale lodging
for luxury yachts and people near Fort Mason.

▲ Ferries have plied the waters of the San
Francisco Bay for more than 150 years, providing necessary
transportation for commuters as well as pleasure tours for visitors.
▶ An oil tanker leaves the Bay for ports unknown. The Bay is
a natural harbor that connects to destinations along
the West Coast as well as ports worldwide.

◄ Flamingos are just one of the approximately
250 species that are housed at the San Francisco Zoo.
▲ Dolores Park, in the Mission Dolores neighborhood, offers
picnic areas, tennis courts, a basketball court, a children's
playground—and free concerts from time to time.

▲ This cast of *The Thinker*, by Auguste Rodin, occupies a
prominent place in the courtyard of the California Palace of the
Legion of Honor. It was purchased for the museum by Alma Spreckels,
known as the great-grandmother of San Francisco. The museum houses
more than eighty-seven thousand works of art of various types,
some as much as four thousand years old.

▲ The Palace of the Legion of Honor was
designed as a three-quarters imitation (not an
exact copy) of the Palais de la Légion d'Honneur
in Paris. It was built to honor the thirty-six hundred
California soldiers who died during World War I.

▲ Grace Cathedral was actually founded in 1849 during the gold rush.
The third church was destroyed in the fire following the 1906 earthquake.
Work began on the present cathedral in 1928 and was completed in 1964.

▶ The Westfield San Francisco Centre, an upscale shopping mall, first opened
in 1988. The mall features the first spiral escalators in the United States.

▶▶ Alcatraz was *the* top security prison from the mid-1930s until the
mid-1960s, housing the most incorrigible of America's criminals.

◄ The entrance to Chinatown is
marked by lions under a distinctly Chinese arch.
▲ Chinese lanterns brighten historic Chinatown, established
in the 1850s. Though today several neighborhoods sport Chinese
architecture, food, and atmosphere, more people still visit
historic Chinatown than the Golden Gate Bridge.

▲ California Street exemplifies the
steep hills so prevalent in San Francisco.
▶ The San Francisco Asian Art Museum, opened in
1966, has collected more than seventeen thousand artworks
spanning six thousand years of history. An exhibit of the art of
the Ming Dynasty was a major attraction in 2008.

◄ The North (Dutch) Windmill was restored in 1980,
when the adjacent Queen Wilhelmina Tulip Garden was planted.
▲ Visitors enjoy a respite in the courtyard of the San Francisco
Art Institute, a school of art offering bachelor's and
master's degrees in arts and fine arts.

▲ Opened in 1915, San Francisco's present City Hall
replaced an earlier City Hall that was destroyed by the 1906 earthquake.
▶ The Korean community's annual cultural picnic in Golden Gate
Park includes performances by dancers and musicians.

◄ The 210-foot-tall Coit Tower was built in 1933
on top of Telegraph Hill at the bequest of Lillie Coit.
▲ Originally acquired in 1893 as headquarters for the
Ghirardelli Chocolate Company, the site was converted
in the 1960s to a restaurant and shopping complex.
►► North Beach is a vibrant neighborhood
known for arts, crafts, and jazz festivals.

▲ The parish school of Saints Peter and
Paul Church is unusual; it sits atop the church itself
and is accessible from stairways under each of its twin towers.
► San Francisco has sixteen skyscrapers rising at least five hundred
feet in height, with two more under construction.
►► The Esplanade stretches south from
the historic Ferry Building.

◄ The Embarcadero Center, home to great
shopping, dining, and entertainment, encompasses
five blocks in the heart of San Francisco's commercial district.
▲ Colorful trolley cars and buses crisscross
the Embarcadero District.

◄ Fog—which threatens to swallow up the
Golden Gate Bridge—backdrops the Palace of Fine Arts.
▲ A detail of one of the pillars of the Palace of Fine Arts depicts
the care that went into creating this beautiful building for
the 1915 Panama-Pacific International Exposition.

▲ The Haight District became famous for the
hippie culture of the 1960s that once defined it.
▶ Lombard Street, San Francisco's—and America's—
"crookedest street," with switchbacks lined with curving,
flower-covered hedges, is situated on a steep hillside.

◄ Transamerica Pyramid, completed in 1972,
houses some fifty firms, including the Transamerica
Corporation, an investment and insurance company. The
historic Sentinel Building, the "flatiron"-style building next to the
Pyramid, is home to Francis Ford Coppola's American Zoetrope studio.
▲ An aerial view of the Transamerica Building clearly shows
the pyramid shape, designed to withstand earthquakes.

▲ Double backflips and jumping over hurdles are almost
routine for the trick bikes at the X Games, held in different locations
each year. They took place in San Francisco in 2000, near the Embarcadero.
▶ Near Pier 39, the Embarcadero is filled with shoppers and tourists.
▶▶ Since its founding in 1984, the Contemporary Jewish Museum
has explored contemporary perspectives on Jewish
culture, history, art, and ideas.

The sign reads:

PIER 39

Harassment of the
Sea Lions is a Violation
of the Marine Mammal
Protection Act.
No Docking,
Approaching, Feeding
or Throwing
Objects Allowed.

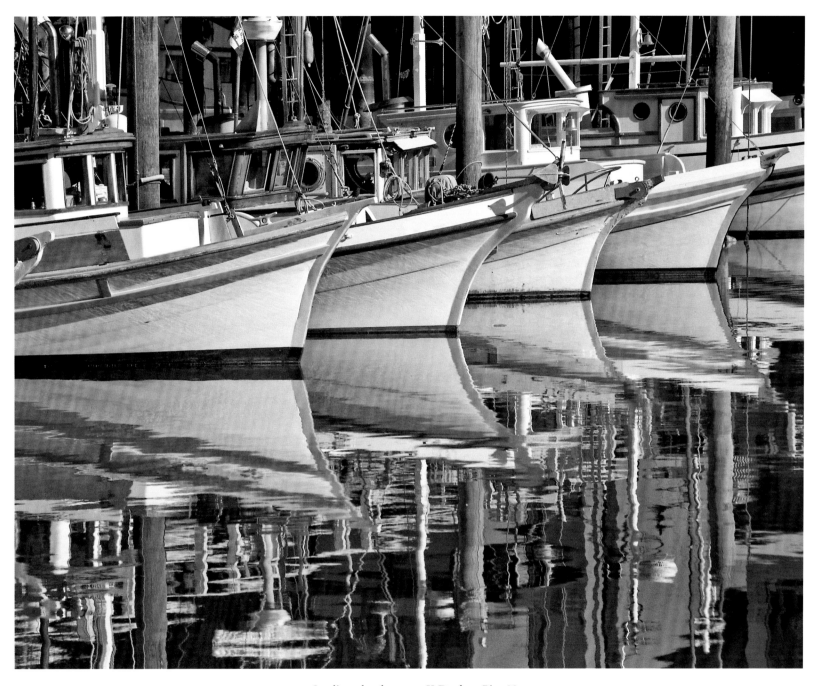

◀ Sea lions haul out on K Dock at Pier 39.
Pier 39 is also famous for other attractions, including
street entertainers, waterfront dining, and shopping.
▲ Colorful small boats line the dock of a marina.

◀ The Chinese New Year Parade is one of only
a handful of illuminated parades in the United States.
▲ A children's marching band participates in
the Chinese New Year Parade.

◄ A local transport MUNI
train stops at the Embarcadero.
▲ The Main Library is the resource center for the
city's library system as well as for all of northern California.
►► It doesn't get better than this: fishing off the dock at Fort
Mason, with a sailboat catching the breeze in the Bay.

◄ A fire escape zigzags down
the side of an apartment building.
▲ Mission Dolores Church, the oldest building
in San Francisco, was founded as Misión San Francisco
de Asís in June 1776 by Father Junípero Serra.

▲ A sixty-foot-tall bow and arrow decorates
Rincon Park. Called *Cupid's Span,* it was created by
Claes Oldenburg and Coosje van Bruggen.

▲ The Louise M. Davies Symphony Hall
opened in 1980 at a cost of twenty-eight million
dollars. Louise Davies gave five million of those dollars to provide
a permanent home for the San Francisco Symphony.

▲ A young Vietnamese-American boy studies calligraphy.

▶ TOP TO BOTTOM: ◖ City Hall, constructed to replace an
earlier building destroyed in the 1906 earthquake, opened in 1915.
◖ The City Hall Rotunda, which rises 307 feet above the surrounding
area, includes four hundred thousand dollars' worth of gold leaf in its design.
▶▶ The Bay Bridge, a toll bridge connecting San Francisco and
Oakland, carries some 280,000 vehicles each day.

◄ Children rip down the slide at the
children's playground in Golden Gate Park.
▲ Juneteenth is a yearly festival celebrating the
freedom and culture of African-Americans through
music, parades, performing arts, and other activities.
►► Laser sailboaters are backdropped by a fog-
softened Golden Gate Bridge.

▲ With fishing boats docked alongside, Tarantino's, at
Fisherman's Wharf, is a hot spot for those seeking seafood.
▶ A windsurfer enjoys challenging the breeze in the Bay.
▶▶ San Francisco plays host to Fiesta Filipina, the
biggest Filipino festival in America.

◄ The Bay Bridge provides backdrop
for a music concert at the Ferry Terminal.
▲ Greens Restaurant at Fort Mason overlooks the
Marina. Fort Mason is situated between Fisherman's Wharf
and the Golden Gate Bridge on San Francisco Bay.

▲ The skyline from the
Haight District appears ghostlike
through the fog.

▲ A golfer takes on the greens at Lincoln Park,
an eighteen-hole course that has been offering exercise and
fun to San Franciscans for some seventy-five years.

▲ Fun with color is just one of the
many hands-on exhibits at the Exploratorium.
► On a clear day, the San Francisco skyline is visible
from the town of Sausalito, across the Bay to the north.
►► For 218 years the Presidio served as an army post for the
soldiers of three nations—Spain, Mexico, and the United States. In 1994,
it became a part of the Golden Gate National Recreation Area.

◄ Ocean Beach, along San Francisco's west coast,
is part of the Golden Gate National Recreation Area.
▲ Beachgoers enjoy the view of crashing waves in the
small cove at McClures Beach at Point Reyes.

▲ Among the features at Yerba Buena are the
Moscone Convention Center, the Metreon (a Sony
entertainment center), and the Yerba Buena Center for the Arts.
Situated on the rooftop are activities ranging from year-round ice-skating
and bowling to a playground and an interactive museum.

▲ The Yerba Buena Gardens, San Francisco's
"front yard," encompass five and one-half acres of natural
beauty, complemented by sculptures and waterfalls.

▲ A martial art student shows his moves at the Asian Heritage Street
Fair, held in San Francisco's Japantown on the third Saturday of May each year.
► Baker Beach offers a magnificent view of the Golden Gate Bridge.
►► The Bay Bridge, officially known as the San Francisco–
Oakland Bay Bridge, opened for traffic in 1936. Its
spans rest in the middle of Yerba Buena Island.

◄ North Beach—sometimes known
as San Francisco's Little Italy—is a popular
neighborhood rich with arts, crafts, music, and restaurants.
▲ A military installation until the 1960s, today Fort Mason features parks,
gardens, and the Fort Mason Center, which hosts thousands of
events, fairs, exhibits, and performances each year.

▲ A beautiful Japanese Tea Garden graces Golden Gate Park.
► CLOCKWISE FROM TOP LEFT: Japantown offers much to see:
● A Japanese American dancer performing classical Japanese dance;
● A young girl exhibiting quintessential Japanese dress; and
● Sumo wrestlers competing in a traditional match.

98

◄ The Old St. Mary's Cathedral, dedicated in 1854,
survived the earthquake of 1906 only to be gutted by the fire that
roared through the city. The renovated church was dedicated in 1909.
▲ The San Francisco Maritime National Historical Park, situated
near Fisherman's Wharf, displays historical vessels, including
the 1886 square-rigged ship *Balclutha*.

▲ San Francisco International Airport
is the second-busiest airport in California, and
the thirteenth-busiest in the United States.

▲ An arts and crafts market attracts customers
at the foot of Market Street, an important arterial
in the city throughout San Francisco's history. Over the
years, it has carried horse-drawn streetcars, cable cars, electric
streetcars, electric trolleybuses, and diesel buses.

▲ AT&T Park is home to the San Francisco Giants. An unusual
feature of the ballpark is that all seats face the baseball diamond.
▶ Opened in 1935, the San Francisco Museum of Modern Art is the only
West Coast museum limited to art of the twentieth and twenty-first centuries.
▶▶ A Coast Guard vessel, motorboats, small sailing boats, and tall
ships—the Bay sees all kinds of recreational vessels.

◄ Important not only as a botanical greenhouse,
the Conservatory of Flowers is also important historically.
Constructed in 1878, it is the oldest building in Golden Gate Park.
▲ The first Cliff House, built in 1863, was destroyed by fire in 1894. In 1907,
the second also succumbed to fire. The present Cliff House was constructed in 1909
and is now preserved as part of the Golden Gate National Recreation Area.
►► The de Young Museum is the city's largest public arts institution.

▲ The #9 Fishermen's Grotto, which has been in operation since 1935, was the first sit-down restaurant on Fisherman's Wharf.

▶ Columbus Avenue, in the northern part of Chinatown, bustles with traffic at night.

▶▶ The Transamerica Pyramid and the Golden Gate Bridge form an interesting collage. The pyramid is the kingpin of the Transamerica Center, a complex that includes Two Transamerica Center and Transamerica Redwood Park.